Thunder Cave

Written by Jenny Feely
Illustrated by Chantal Stewart

Flying Start
to Literacy®

T0363492

Contents

Chapter 1
Watch out at Thunder Cave

"Where are you off to today?" Rick asked my dad as he wrapped up the bait we'd just bought.

"I thought we'd go down to Thunder Cave," said Dad. "I hear the fish are really biting there."

We'd been to Thunder Cave before, but never to fish. It was an amazing place. Usually we went in the winter when the sea was stormy and the waves crashed into the cave, making a loud rumbling noise – just like thunder. That was how the cave got its name.

Right next to Thunder Cave was a rocky platform that jutted out into the sea. This was a great place to fish because just next to the rocks, the water was very deep and there were lots of fish.

"Ah, the fish love it down there," said Rick, "but you want to watch out. Thunder Cave can be a dangerous place to go fishing."

"What do you mean?" I asked.

"People have gone fishing at Thunder Cave and have been washed off the rocks," said Rick. "And they have never been seen again. You have to be careful down there."

My stomach did a nervous little jiggle.

"Don't worry about us," said Dad. "Thunder Cave is only dangerous when the sea is rough and there are big waves. It's calm today, so we'll be safe. And the fish will be biting!"

"Well, you know what they say," said Rick. "Never turn your back on the sea. Make sure you watch out at Thunder Cave."

Chapter 2
A forest full of fish

Usually you can hear Thunder Cave before you see it, but today the only sounds were the seagulls squawking and a gentle slap, slap, as the small waves moved in and out. But I couldn't stop thinking about what Rick had said about the people being washed off the rocks.

"Dad," I said, "maybe we should just fish off the beach today."

"Why?" said Dad. "Fishermen go where the fish are. And today I reckon the fish are at Thunder Cave."

I didn't want Dad to think I was scared, so I just smiled and nodded.

To get to Thunder Cave, we had to walk down some steps and then climb down a ladder onto the rocks. When we got there, we saw some huge pieces of driftwood washed up on the rocks.

"I've never seen driftwood on these rocks before," said Dad. "A big wave must have brought this in."

Rick's words raced through my head – "Watch out at Thunder Cave". I swallowed and put the bait on the hook.

"Where do you think I should fish?" I asked Dad.

"Try over there. Just stay out of the channel that runs into Thunder Cave," said Dad. "It's full of kelp and your fishing line will get tangled."

I've never liked seaweed – not since I got bitten by a crab while walking through a small patch of it at the beach. I looked at the kelp. It was so thick and dark that you couldn't see down into the water.

"Where did all that kelp come from?" I asked. "It wasn't there last time we came."

"That's because it was winter then. Winter storms rip the kelp off the rocks. But when the spring comes, it all grows back again. And now it's summer, the kelp has grown so much that it is like a forest under the sea."

"Well, I don't like it," I said.

"Well, you should," said Dad. "That's why this is such a good place to fish. That kelp forest attracts all the fish because that's where they shelter. When they come out into the open water to catch food, we can catch them!"

We cast out near the kelp and began to fish. But I couldn't take my eyes off the kelp. Its thick leaves reached out over the water like fingers waiting to catch things – catch them and pull them into the deep, dark water. And that was when Dad yelled, "Look out!"

Chapter 3

A big one

"You've got a fish on your hook," said Dad.
And I did!

I pulled and pulled and wound the line back
in as fast as I could. Soon I had a glittering
silver fish in my net.

"I knew the fish would be biting here today,"
said Dad.

Soon we were catching fish almost as quickly as we could throw the hooks into the water. I was so busy putting bait on my hook and reeling in fish that I didn't notice that the waves were getting bigger.   But Dad did.

"It's time to get off these rocks," he said. "I can see a big set of waves coming in, and it pays to be careful."

I quickly climbed up the ladder and Dad started to pass all our fishing gear up to me.

A big wave came rolling in.

Boom! went Thunder Cave as the wave hit. I watched as three more came in.

Boom! Boom! Boom!

Dad was still passing gear up to me. From the top of the ladder I saw three more big waves coming – and behind them was a huge monster of white water, headed straight for us!

"Quick!" I yelled. "There's a huge wave coming!"

"Leave the stuff!" Dad yelled, as he started to climb up the ladder.

Boom!

I headed for the steps.

Boom!

I looked back to see Dad's head at the top of the ladder.

Boom!

Up the steps I went.

Boom!

There was a mighty noise as the huge wave crashed into Thunder Cave. Water splashed up the steps, soaking me all over. I turned around. Where was Dad?

"Dad!" I screamed. But he was gone.

Chapter 4

Washed away?

I charged back down the steps and to the ladder, but the waves were still crashing onto it.   I couldn't climb down!

"Dad! Dad! Dad!"

Over and over I called. My eyes searched the waves for him, but I couldn't see him anywhere. I didn't know what to do. I looked around for help but there was no one in sight. Maybe I should run back to Rick's to get help, I thought, but I didn't want to leave Dad, and it would take too long. I had to do something, and now!

My heart was pounding in my chest. Rick had warned us about Thunder Cave.

We should have listened to him, I thought to myself. Please don't let it be too late! Please let Dad be okay!

Finally, the waves started to die down.
I scrambled down the ladder and looked
around. No Dad.

"Dad!" I called at the top of my lungs.
"Where are you?"

I looked at the kelp. Smaller waves were
coming in now as if nothing had happened,
and the mass of dark kelp was rising up
and down. If Dad had got caught in
the kelp – would he be able to survive?

I looked down at the rocks and felt tears
welling in my eyes. Dad was missing and
there was nothing I could do. I needed to
find help. I started toward the ladder.

And that's when I heard something.

"Keira, Keira. I'm over here – in the kelp!"

It was Dad's voice. I looked into the kelp. There he was! He looked like he was floating on top of the kelp. Long strands of kelp were wrapped around his legs.

"I'm tangled in the kelp!" he yelled.

"I'll try to get you out!" I called. "I can reach you with a fishing rod."

I looked around to grab a rod, but our fishing gear had been washed away by the big wave.

Then I saw a piece of driftwood. I ran and grabbed it and dragged it back. I got down low to the ground and pushed the driftwood out over the kelp to Dad.

Dad grabbed the driftwood and untangled
himself from the kelp. He used the
driftwood to keep himself afloat until he
reached the rocks. And then Dad was
hugging me and everything was all right.

Chapter 5

Saved by the kelp

We headed back to Rick's bait shop. When Dad walked through the door, Rick was shocked.

"What happened to you?" he asked.

I told Rick what had happened while he patched Dad up.

"But how did you survive?" Rick asked Dad.

"When I got washed off the rocks, I grabbed the kelp," said Dad. "I lay on the top of it and wrapped it around my legs. It stopped me from getting washed out to sea."

"You sure are one lucky fisherman," said Rick.

And from then on, whenever Rick told people about Thunder Cave, he said, "Watch out at Thunder Cave. Some people have been washed off the rocks and never seen again. But one of the luckiest fishermen I ever met was saved by the kelp."

A note from the author

This story is based on the real-life adventures of my friend Helen's father, who was washed into a very dangerous blowhole by a freak wave. Blowholes are rocky holes that the waves rush into with thunderous crashes, spraying water high up into the air.
Six fishermen had drowned in this blowhole and when Helen's dad was washed off the rocks and into the blowhole, he thought he would die. But luckily he was able to save himself by wrapping himself in the kelp that grew in the blowhole.

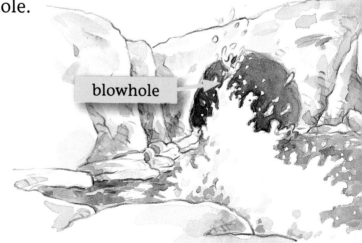

blowhole